About the Author

Timothy Raphael Phillips was born in Leeds but spent very little time there before he was nine years old. Having come from an artistic family, he felt almost obliged to find a talent— firstly art, then music, playing drums, and writing songs with band members. Maybe this is what started his journey into poetry. In the mid-90s, after his first marriage failed, he became inspired to release his thoughts and worries through poetry. Since retiring and having a second divorce, his writing flourished, no doubt as a result of having more thinking time. Life on his boat, 'Sophie' has certainly helped in his productivity.

To MARTIN.

ENJOY

One Hundred Plus Musings of Pride, Peace, Pain & Passion

Timothy Raphael Phillips

One Hundred Plus Musings of Pride, Peace, Pain & Passion

Olympia Publishers
London

www.olympiapublishers.com
OLYMPIA PAPERBACK EDITION

A CIP catalogue record for this title is
available from the British Library.

ISBN: 978-1-83543-051-4

This is a work of fiction.
Names, characters, places and incidents originate from the writer's
imagination. Any resemblance to actual persons, living or dead, is
purely coincidental.

First Published in 2024

Olympia Publishers
Tallis House
2 Tallis Street
London
EC4Y 0AB

Printed in Great Britain

Dedication

My writing, as always, is dedicated to the people around me who keep me sane and grounded with their friendship and love, but particularly to my mum Frances, who died in 2014, and of course to my son Sebastian and daughter Kate, who continually add colour and joy to my life.

Acknowledgements

Thank you to Facebook, Dominique and Michelle for the inspiration to get a book together.

Foreword

Poetry

There's something in writing verse that allows my brain to
thrive,
Like walking in sunshine with one you love and feeling so
alive.
Expressing myself in poetry often takes me by surprise,
Words springing into my head as the cogs whir deep inside.
I begin with an image or a thought sprung from my heart,
Forming what I want to say and thinking about where to start.
The flow comes quickly as I start to write, matching words
and rhyme,
The picture I paint fills my mind with colour as I capture a
moment in time.

What Makes Me?

At three-thirty a.m., most sound-minded people and probably those less sound or lucky in life will be fast asleep, their bodies recharging the brain cells for the next day's challenges.

Me? I'm not sure everyone would consider me sound of mind and I'm not asleep and recharging. Those who know me well have expressed their admiration for my grit, stamina, empathy, determination, practicality, passion, enthusiasm, positivity, and various achievements in my life.

At this ungodly hour, I find myself delving into my psyche and finding the things from my past that have influenced me with hope that I gain an understanding of how to ensure the path ahead is smooth. Develop the good, learn from the bad, so to speak.

What made me then?

Dealing healthily with loss is something I feel is one of my greatest strengths. I'm emotionally affected and feel pain, but this subsides quickly to be taken over by inspiration and release.

Remembering significant things about someone is something that I find easy; maybe the inspiration from this gives me strength.

My earliest memory is of my father, Jon Phillips, leaving. My mum Fran gave him an ultimatum (he lacked self-motivation at this time and wasn't contributing to the family), and he decided to go.

I watched him walk away wearing a cowboy hat and carrying his guitar and a suitcase. I wanted to see his face, but he never looked back.

Taking care of my brother Tristram was something that became instinct, often fighting his battles (he seemed to get himself into trouble a lot) feeling his pain or suffering (I cried when he got stung by a bee) and involving him in all my play. It wasn't until he started to want his own independence that I let go of my grasp on his well-being. We keep in touch irregularly and he often compares me to our father, but he is the "chip off the old block", so to speak, being very similar to Jon.

My mum quickly met Roy Warne, who became our second dad. When my brother Nicholas was born, Roy took Tristram and I to a fairground to entertain us whilst Mum was busy giving birth. I wanted a go in the dodgems, but Roy took us to a roundabout-style ride with cars, etc that went around an undulating road. I can't remember a fairground ride before this, I was five and looking after my little brother of course so when he started crying, I did. We got taken off the ride and Roy refused to let us do any others.

I realise now that he couldn't cope with children's behaviour, lacking the empathy to see what had happened. When my mum sent Tristram and I to stay with my father for a while a couple of years later (a hugely exciting adventure for us both), we had no idea it was because Roy couldn't cope with having us around as well as his own son Nicholas.

We never went back to live with my mum.

My father asked us to live with him and his then-girlfriend Janet, my second mum. Tristram and I loved Janet, who treated and mothered us as if her own. He and Janet got divorced after she found out he was having an affair with Monica, who ended up being my third mum. Janet stayed in the house in Headingley for a while after throwing my father out. It broke her heart to see my brother and I go too.

My mum Fran was very different, she instinctively knew what was wrong and some of my fondest, if slightly disturbing memories are of her showing such empathy.

We were sat watching a film one evening when I couldn't sleep. The sofa was leather and creaked when you moved so I was sat very still, captivated by the story on the screen. A woman thought she had lost the love of her life in a storm and then found him, in a scene where she ran towards a lighthouse with waves crashing against rocks. Dramatic stuff, as I kept looking at my mum and then the TV screen. When the woman grasped the man and she was swept up in his arms, my mum shuddered. I felt tears in my eyes and tried to wipe them away, but one fell and splatted on the leather sofa! My mum turned to me with eyes full of tears, realised I was crying because she was, and gave me a big hug, lifting me up. "Aw Tim, c'mon, let's go to bed," she wept, her smile telling me that everything was all right really.

My brother Tristram and I were sat on our doorstep a few months later, in early spring, quite cold, shivering, and not allowed to go in because Mum was sorting out and cleaning the house.

We were knocking on the door, asking to come in, when it opened. My brother and I quickly stood up expecting to get told off. My mum appeared with a concerned smile on her face, holding a plate full of toasted and buttered hot cross buns for us. "Won't be long now, boys. When you've eaten these, you can come in." That was one of the best moments.

So, what made her give us up?

There were so many memories for me in that household with Roy and Nicholas. Firstly, in Hampstead Heath, then a cottage in Brindle, Lancashire, then in nearby Withnell on a farm.

Going to the shops with a three-penny bit for sweets, playing with Gollywogs mum had made us.

Watching a woman pee standing up and then realising Roland, a close family friend, was in fact a man dressed in woman's clothes.

Seeing a man whose face was covered in blood be pulled out of his car that crashed right across from our house.

Helping Roy with decorating the farmhouse before we moved in and having to drink black tea because that's all he'd brought.

Sitting crying on Christmas morning with a piece of my new bike in my hand which I thought I'd broken. Of course, the tears disappeared when Mum came down and put the piece back on easily.

Eating blackened spit-roasted sheep and baked potatoes at a party my parents held for friends at the farm.

Digging for hours in the huge garden where my best buddy Goldie (Golden Labrador) was buried because I missed her terribly.

I could go on, but you get my drift. Many events that started to mould me into who I've become.

My mum was never able to explain clearly why she sent my brother and I to live with my father. She regretted how weak she'd been in her relationship with Roy, how she'd struggled with her emotions after my brother Nick was born, and that passing us over to my father seemed an easy way out.

I understood this and accepted it quite early in my teens. Yes, my life could have been different. There were things I hated about living with my father (most teens go through this stage in life), but my strength in tricky situations and my ability to think quickly and persevere to find a solution probably stem from the need to adapt, cope and protect when I was young.

What of my father?

I haven't spoken to Jon since my son Sebastian (Seb to his friends) was seven. He attended Seb's birthday party we held at Harewood House, was quite distant and obviously uncomfortable around my new family and since then hasn't acknowledged his grandson's progression in life; despite my early attempts to involve him.

When my daughter Kate was born, I tried that day to pass on my joyous news and invited him to visit us. His conversation quickly diverted to some toy he'd found for Sebastian. I thanked him but pointed out that Seb was sixteen and probably wouldn't be into that sort of thing now.
Kate has never met her grandfather on my side of the family.

Recently, Sebastian decided he wanted to contact Jon, seeing him once, with my brother and cousin, over a year ago after being in the hospital, and Seb rang him a few weeks ago to see how he was. Jon wouldn't think to contact anyone in his family unless there was something he wanted.
He's only met my brother Tristram's family once and doesn't stay in touch with any of my uncles and aunts.

My mum, on the other hand, despite hating talking on the phone, would keep in touch regularly and loved having her whole family stay during the holidays. We made some fantastic memories on the beach in Whitstable, where she had a lovely cottage.

This contrast in my parents' involvement in my life leaves me with both regret that I didn't spend enough time with my mum and a lack of respect for my father whose actions showed me that he really doesn't care for anybody but himself. I have no other emotions for him; I certainly don't hate him, but I don't think I have ever loved him like I did my mum, my stepfather Neil Slings by (may one of the nicest men I've ever met rest in peace), and the few family members I have left who thankfully stay in touch via Facebook.

When my mum was dying, I was heartbroken and luckily was given leave to be with her and my brother in that time of need. I don't think I'm going to be affected in that way when my father passes.

When did this start?

I can't ever remember admiration or affection for my father or his actions. He kept a roof over our heads and involved us in things he wanted to do but never played with my brother, stepbrother, Dominic and me.

After visiting him for birthdays and Christmas, I was always left feeling disappointed with events and the only things I really enjoyed with him were music and food. As my Uncle David once said, you needed degrees in several subjects to keep up with my father's conversations and quite often he went on about things that were obviously not interesting to anyone but him.

Eventually, my father found religion, being baptised in a gospel church, and rediscovered his love for playing music. He's an excellent guitarist when he applies himself. Of course, like everything else he did in life, he went at being "Born again" one thousand per cent, talking and preaching about nothing else each time we met. Tedious and uninviting are two words that spring to mind.

This, coupled with the other things I've mentioned, were nails in the coffin of our relationship, me being an atheist 'n' all.

So why am I thinking of all this now?

My life has changed so much in the last year that I want to let the world around me know that good things are happening and I'm the happiest I've ever been. Challenges have arisen in the last couple of years; I've been hurt, both physically and mentally, and sometimes I think about what-ifs, could-have-beens, and maybes.

Despite this, my outlook on life ahead remains bright and full of promise that my retirement will be what I've always wanted it to be; relaxed, enjoyable, challenging mentally and physically, and shared with someone I truly love. I'm getting there, but as far as writing is concerned, my reflections keep on coming. Memories make life more enjoyable but also bring back pain. If you like my poems, then the pain is worth it.

All the below have been previously posted on Facebook.

Why the Net

Saturday, 9 October 2021
12:09

I thought about my joy of writing and photography and how sad it would be if nobody shared and enjoyed what I had to offer. Before the internet and the cloud, sharing what I was inspired with took a whole lot more time and effort, selecting, printing, sending to publishers, and then circulating in the impossibly difficult world of media at that time.

Having the ability to put your inspiration straight out there for others to see, like, comment on, and share is so self-motivating and easy that I find it very hard to understand why it should be the source of derision for some. Are they afraid of being misunderstood by others? Maybe they feel that the old ways were better or more robust.

Well, if you feel that way, get off the internet, social media, your smartphone, etc., and get back into your cave! The way we now communicate is here to stay and will probably become faster and easier as time goes on.

I have always believed in self-expression, in whatever form that takes. If other people like what I say, like, do, and experience, then good for you; I'm happy to continue enriching your lives in any way I can.

If you don't like it, then don't follow me, read my stuff, look at my pictures, or comment without any context as to what you're getting at. I'll happily take feedback if it's constructive and comes from someone who I consider knowledgeable in that field.

I love social media, particularly Facebook, as an avenue for expressing who I am. I admire all those who use social media as it should be used; for communicating good, love, and positive unity to those around them.

Pride

There have been many things in my life that have made me proud of who I am, how I've lived, and how I express myself. Being able to write about them has helped others to understand me and certainly aided in building my relationships with friends and family who have all inspired me.

A God-Given Gift?

Thursday, 4 November 2021
15:48

Can we call writing a God-given gift?
Emotions stirring so many hearts to lift.
Thoughts on paper stimulating the mind,
Feelings remembered, so they stick with time.

What really inspires such heartfelt poem?
Surely a relationship, full and growing.
The strength of love smoothly flowing in ink,
Words coming seamlessly, not having to think.

Could it be that music created such rhyme?
Beating to the rhythm like the heart of time.
Experiencing previously subdued senses,
Powerfully enhancing unceasing intenseness.

Is it the fact that you're reading these words?
An insight into something maybe wild or unheard.
Developing a pattern that twists and turns,
A fire fuelled by memories of a passion that burns.

Can we say what compels anyone to write?
Illustrating pictures from thoughts, sounds, and sights.
Throwing light on how your feelings shift,
Is writing really a God-given gift?

Spring into Life

31.01.2017

The "Brexit" and Donald Trump era was pending.

It's clear that the voice of the world is alight,
With a fire stoked high by democracy's plight.

As we trudge through the misery of winter's ails,
The power of the people seems doomed to fail.

Can we be heard amidst the noise of fear,
And protect those whose love we hold so dear?

Be as it may, we must not lose all hope,
For humanity has a habit of being able to cope.

As the climate warms the earths blooms to spring
Human spirit will prevail with life to sing.

Home Late

Tuesday, 10 November 2020
21:56

This was written after my first cruise on Sophie, which ended up being three months, rather than the planned three weeks, after being stranded for two months in the Pennines above Manchester.

It's been hard, a trial of body, mind, hardiness, and perseverance.
There've been times when I wished that turning left was not the choice.

I've seen things, the like of which could make you weep or dance.
My body cried with the pain of failing to hear common sense's voice.

Sometimes it felt that all seemed to go against the flow.
Yet still I tried, fighting that urge to give in easily to fate.

Counting the days as time slowly edged to the day I could go.
Homeward bound, grafting with new urgency to arrive so late.

Tween

Growing pains ache to the core,
Restlessness feels like a chore.
Anxiety that the whole world's ignored,
Fed up with the workload to endure.

Hormones play games with the core,
Getting out of bed becomes a chore.
Stressing about which advice gets ignored,
A labyrinth of emotions to endure.

Frustration takes hold of the core,
Climbing a mountain to complete every chore.
Complaints just seem to be ignored,
Slow pace, dragging out what's to endure.

A warm embrace calms the woes inner core,
Suddenly, life's not so much of a chore.
As the voice seems no longer to be ignored,
Motivation sparks a will to endure.

Son

Saturday, 19 December 2020
15:38

First written in 1997 when my son was five years old.

You are the sun that shines,
Joyously, gloriously, every day.
You fill my heart with pride,
In your love, in song, in play.

I feel your smile and hear,
Fantastic things you say.
And wonder at your mind and
The splendour of your ways.

You are the son that shines,
For all with love for thee.
You fill their hearts with pride,
For everything in you, they see.

Sophie

I love the mechanical sounds of my boat waking up.

The rhythmic whirring of pumps and cogs brings magical images to my mind of a futuristic world within which I now live.

Love of this life was something I dreamt about for a long time and was lucky to fulfil. Having this space gives me a satisfaction that I can be myself, create, love, and thrive.

The feeling of security inside my steel shell provides comfort amid the turmoil of a world fraught with uncertainty and fear; I'm fortunate for being able to shut this out.

My boat moves with me as I go about my day; swaying as I step to wash, dress, cook, listen, dance, and play; even when on land, my ears balance out the motions in my mind.

Sophie purrs as she cruises with a line that gives confidence to a novice hand; quick to react and assuredly efficient in her use of power through locks, bridge, and the cut.

Mooring up, she creaks quietly as my routine puts her to bed for the night; secured in the knowledge that she'll protect me until the dawning of another adventure in my floating life.

Green

Saturday, 2 January 2021
23:13

Published in an anthology by Forward Press 1999 - TR Phillips —
Poets in Passing

Green is the colour of life,
Green gives us food and warmth.
Green tells us when we are right,
Green indicates to go forth.

Green can be darker than black,
Green of shades almost white.
Green fills our world with splendour,
Green shows off power and might.

Green is the pride of most homes,
Green the bearer of delights.
Green backs up all beauty,
Green shines through even night.

Green is the colour of peace,
Green a sanctuary for lost souls.
Green leaves, well-tended, shine with youth,
Green left to rot will grow mould.

Green an enemy from within,
Green with jealousy for our fellows.
Green is our illness and sin,
Green the water of the shallow.

Green is the colour of life!
Green the food for good health.
Green fruits from long, hard strife,
Green the richness of all wealth.

Monster Mash

Monday, 12 April 2021
13:56

To my wonderful uncle Adrian - RIP

Great Granny Georgia lived near Lewes Castle in a lovely old house called Moat Cottage.
My first memory of Uncle Adrian was playing there with Tristram and I, at God knows what age.
I can't remember much of our play but remember our laughter and his beaming smile.
Singing "The Monster Mash" and chasing us, giggling, and screaming around the house for a while.

The attic room at Grandma Kae's was our favourite place when Uncle Adrian came to stay.
Up a secret stair into a dark wood room filled with boxes of wonder to while time away.
We'd play with tin soldiers and sailors Grandpa Harry had made to sail on great ships.
"Play nicely, children," Grandma would say, as we held great battles with huge smiles on our lips.

Adrian told us about Napoleon fighting Nelson and the Battle of Waterloo.

He recalled all the names of the captains and about boats
knew a thing or two.
He enthralled us with stories of his childhood, painting
soldiers with Uncle Steve.
Of my father eating loaves of bread after family dining at the
table, he'd asked to leave.

As I grew older, Adrian's storytelling kept us rapt when the
adults rambled on.
Despite rarely seeing him, my Uncle Adrian and his smile will
be a memory never gone.

Read by me at his funeral.

Jungle Taking Over

08 November 2019
12:55

Goldie was the first that stirred my blood,
Timeless explosions to hook me good.
My ears ringing with Saturn's refrain,
Breaking drum and bass to frazzle one's brain.

Shy FX me then with the way I dance,
Thanks to Stacy and our nights of trance.
Old school freestyler to fix my moves,
Banging out bass and drums to a groove.

Finding the Prodigy simply blew my mind,
Those memories of madness, the punk rock kind.
My son Seb got hooked in our chase to new sounds,
Inspired by Congo Natty and the Junglists ground.

We've shared the love of good production,
Danced all night without age restriction.
Almost three decades on and I'm still a mover,
Life treats anyone submitting to jungle taking over.

Drums

Saturday, 22 May 2021
15:39

Listening to Killing Joke, "What's This For?" Wishing I could fit my
acoustic kit on the boat!

Clash, bang, wallop, bash!
The angst comes out with an almighty thrash.
Tap, swish, roll, ride,
Rhythm so soft but nowhere to hide.
Crash, bongo, hi-hat, snare,
Timing it right, keep up if you care.
Tinkle, shuffle, rattle, tattle,
Hands and feet creating a musical battle.
Bass, race, trace, deface,
Sticks seem to fly all over the place.
Bounce, flounce, pounce, trounce,
Passion flowing through with every ounce.

Dub

Saturday, 19 June 2021
20:24

*At The Old Red Bus Station (ORBS), Leeds - my imagination
taking over the fact that I have to sit!*

Drums pumping till my heart beats in rhyme,
Snare snapping as if keeping the time.
Hi-hat tap tapping to create the flow,
Bass in sync til I feel it below.

Nodding my head as my instincts take hold,
The rhythm hypnotic as my senses unfold.
Beats becomes stronger as each tune plays,
DJ takes over as the crowd skanks and sways.

Wobbling and squelching, the bass goes deep,
Constantly pounding, the rhythm drums keep.
The mass start bouncing as if they are one,
Moving to the music that has them overcome.

Tune after tune keeps the throng in their trance,
Dub so damn good that no drug can enhance.
Bodies swaying, heads bobbing, it gets so hot,
So relentless the rhythm there's no time to stop.

I Want to Dance

Monday, 28 June 2021
14:14

Listening to my music most of each day,
Nodding and tapping to keep blues at bay.
The bass keeping my heart in rhythm and rhyme,
But missing the sensation of dancing in time.

Thinking of those nights where I let myself go,
Feeling euphoria when you hear tunes you know.
The buzz of the crowd all moving as one,
Smiles on their faces as if all worries have gone.

Dancing with freedom is the best therapy,
Clubbing with my friends, such perfection to me.
The glances and cheers are intoxicating and pure,
Better than any drug or stimulant for sure.

Dreaming of those times, my mind looks ahead,
Wanting this hiatus forced upon us to be dead.
The waiting has been too long, I'm itching to go,
I want to dance and will do soon I know.

Brass Knobs

Sunday, 4 July 2021
18:52

Watching a Steampunk parade for the first time.

Walking with pride in their finery and flair,
Hats tilted back and basking in the stares.
So much effort goes into achieving each look,
The finest detail, no matter the hours it took.

Frills, leather, lacy silks, and the finest weave,
Swashbuckling belts and studs, you wouldn't believe.
Layer upon layer with embroidery and print,
They stand out for miles, no need to squint.

Admiring their characters, I'm left in awe,
Despite seeing many dressed like this before.
Such finesse, pure class, with refined allure,
Brass knobs and flintlocks, winners for sure.

Whitby's Finery and Flair: An Ode to Steampunk Weekend

Tuesday, 27 July 2021
17:22

A tricorn, a trilby, the top hat a tilting, such finery acknowledged with a nod and a smile.

That bowler! Those goggles! Such feathers never wilting! Showing off shiny trinkets maybe not polished for a while.

Laces and dresses flow in the light summer breeze, more beauty to behold than I've ever before known.

Leather, studs, and buckles with swashbuckling flourish, strutting with pride as they parade through the town.

Gentlemen with their ladies, walking proudly side by side, stopping to be admired as each camera does raise.

Ladies with that shadow impress with their style, flaunting their passion for frocks, great hair, and high praise.

Anything goes in this celebration of colour, the dedication, culture, and love is very obvious to perceive.

I'm inspired by the skill, creativity, and honour, this truly is a place one can embrace and believe.

My Lady

So beautiful and fair, my mind swirls in your eyes,
Dressed up to the nines, head held up to the skies.
I soak in your smile with my heart pounding so fast,
My soul soaring higher than ever before in my past.

Proudly holding your hand, I feel elevated inside,
To all who observe, our love just cannot hide.
Your glance makes me skip as your face lights up,
I'm awash with passion I taste from this finest cup.

I hold you close as you look into my eyes,
Your love flowing over me without any disguise.
You bite your lip with such uncontrollable emotion,
My heart feels whole wrapped in your total devotion.

Past the Present

Monday, 27 September 2021
15:16

I awoke one morning in a dream from the past,
Dressed in my finery, and steam-punked to the gills.
It seemed I'd finally reached life's calling at last,
Gleaming with pride, loving new and old thrills.

Walking with my fine lady caressing my arm,
A sense of belonging takes me to great heights.
Glances are noticed as we parade our charm,
Admirations are welcomed as we enjoy the sights.

Feeling this proud reminds me of my youth,
A strutting cockerel out to create great scenes.
Cutting a dash as we journeyed north and south,
Music and culture born from tumultuous teens.

Now my life has given me a greater view,
Maturity and knowledge painting a brighter path.
Showing me a world that I hardly before knew,
Present in a future devoid of stress or wrath.

Everyone Is Awesome

Tuesday, 12 October 2021
13:59

I've lived my life believing that there's good in everyone,
I'm sure there's a bad streak in all but mainly we're awesome.
Given the right motivation, a bright light shines on everyone,
Sharing what they can give to a world filled with awesome.
If we could only see the good, that's abundant inside everyone,
We wouldn't be able to comprehend how we can all be awesome.

My Space

Wednesday, 1 December 2021
12:28

Alone, I'm in my favourite solo place,
Nobody feels the need to interrupt this space.
Music blasts out as I lie back and chill,
Not a care in the world to forget all its ills.

Cosy in my boat with my mind wondering around,
The winter blowing over without audible sound.
I dream of my love and what that brings to my heart,
Great depth in my emotions right from the start.

When I share my space, such contact stays close,
An enjoyment of food and entertainment we chose.
I love the sensations felt with us moving about,
The boat rocking gently as we sing, dance, and shout.

As night draws in, I feel safe within Sophie's hull,
The comforting glow of my stove never gets dull.
My world fills with pleasures as I enjoy my boat,
This idyllic retirement continues to drive life afloat.

Beautiful Soul

Wednesday, 27 July 2022
21:58

My mother was one, though troubled through life,
giving herself without any expectations in return, except love.

I loved her, though troubled through life,
offering her what a mother and grandmother would expect
from such love.

We missed our mum, through our troubles of life,
living with my father, who seemed afraid to show any
semblance of love.

Our beautiful soul, through our troubles of life,
regretting losing us for a relationship that turned out not to
be love.

Dancer

Wednesday, 7 September 2022
22:49

Creating waves like a flickering butterfly,
All her body moves perfectly with each beat.
Delicate fingers pick out the intricate highs,
Rhythm pulses easily from soft-clad feat.

Her smile tells me that she loves this tune,
Eyes closing as each musical climax builds.
Hair shaking gently as her head moves,
Each note giving expression of how she feels.

There's no break in her steps as the DJ flips,
Arms up high as she acknowledges such skill.
Shoulders swaying to the sync of her hips,
The tempo making it impossible to stay still.

Watching the dance, I can't help but smile,
The pleasure of music is plain for all to see.
Keeping time becomes so easy for a while,
I'm in love with dance, the rhythm sets us free.

The Buzz

Saturday, 29 April 2023
16:16

Whilst spending the afternoon in The Potting Shed, Bingley

In anticipation of tomorrow's dancing all night,
My mind's working overtime with what to write.
I'm sat in the pub amidst the hubbub of chat,
Friends talking enthusiastically about this and that.

Laughter and giggles washed down with a tipple,
Watching the interactions as hormones ripple.
Amused by the preening and checking out,
Saturday night flirting is what it's all about.

Spirits are high as the afternoon draws on,
I think about my love and romance just begun.
Happy in the knowledge that my heart is settled,
But enjoying the buzz of those yet unfettered.

Play

When young, my games were played with my brothers,
Battles, explorations, board games, and of course, guns.
We'd build with Lego, Meccano, and many others,
Then destroy with Action Man and tin soldiers for fun.

Television was restricted, so we'd fill our own time,
Racing Scalextric and Matchbox, building them took ages.
Drawing our superheroes, having pen battles in mines,
Making Airfix models, painting then gluing in stages.

As I grew older, my tolerance of games waned,
Girls and music filled my time with great play.
Dancing and kissing were where my passions remained,
Until one day I had a son, then gaming was here to stay.

My experiences as a boy came back to me with ease,
Appreciating that time and effort we'd put into our games.
Seb enjoyed everything and was such a joy to please,
I got to play with toys that as a boy were expensive names.

When Kate came along, I got to do it all again,
She loved Seb's old toys and the games we enjoyed.

Learning how daughters play, an experience that remains,
Dolls, farms, and families, the life skills we employed.

I still love playing all those games that I enjoyed,
Occasionally I find a partner who doesn't mind being beat.
But now puzzle games on my phone keep my mind employed,
As I listen to music and take the weight off my feet.

Peace

Most of the poetry I write comes to me within a few minutes of thinking about an event or what I see and hear. Many are short but all are very personal. Most were liked when they were posted.

Led

Rhythms pulsing til my heart beats in rhyme,
And my soul is carried on the blues of time.
Stinging guitar sends my spirits aloft,
Crashing cymbals stun, then silence so soft.
Crystal harmony rings words sweetly said,
Memories and images of the place we are led.

Music, Poetry for the Soul

Wednesday, 14 October 2020
21:36

I'm listening, my mind keeps wondering around the bass and drum.
Air spinning, highs and lows meandering through the splash and hum.
Keeping me sane, complex rhythms create a rush inside my head.
Breaking the refrain, a tempo change followed by a silence so dead.
Music so pure, my heart sings in harmony on the way to being whole.
Voices so sure, emotions flowing erratically with poetry for the soul.

Mist

Thursday, 26 November 2020
15:49

The sun barely cuts through the trees,
despite there being no leaves.
A haze hangs above water and field,
safe in its low-lying shield.
No wind to blow away the mist,
morning light not warm enough to persist.
Wrapped up snuggly against the chill,
Walking briskly; it's too cold to stay still.

Flakes

Friday, 4 December 2020
13:46

Gloved hands buried deep in my pockets,
Chill winds ache my eyes in their sockets.
Grey skies tell of impending gloom,
Snow on the horizon coming soon.

Fine particles start their meandering fall,
Is it rain? My coat's not wet at all.
A blast peppers my face with its cold,
As flakes get bigger, snow takes hold.

It's too wet on the ground yet to settle,
Quickly melting, even on the coldest metal.
The hills show off their new carpet,
Needs a lot more than this for a blanket.

Christmas

Thursday, 24 December 2020
14:01

For the first time on Christmas Eve, I'm alone,
Yet the feeling of solitude doesn't seem sad.
Memories fill my mind of so many years gone,
My soul is full of loving, there's nothing bad.

For the first time at Christmas, I feel relieved,
There doesn't seem to be the stress of years past.
An acceptance of reality, not what's perceived,
I can't remember when I last felt this relaxed.

For the first time this Christmas, I feel deeply loved,
My heart is given with every emotion I own.
The heavens gave their bounty from high above,
With memories of such love, I'm not alone.

For the first time, Christmas is on my boat,
I'm happy, warm, and stocked with good cheer.
I've grown accustomed to my idyllic space afloat,
Merry Christmas and a Happy New Year!

Before I Awake

Thursday, 6 May 2021
05:24

A hush hangs in my head from this restless night,
An unwillingness to sleep off the anxieties I fight.

My mind whirs with the challenges of life,
How can I be peaceful amongst so much strife?

As birds start to sing the day breaks too slow,
I hope for more sleep, but the wakefulness won't go.

Morning's progression draws inevitably on,
I might as well get up now the sleepless night is gone.

Reflection

Friday, 14 May 2021
16:15

I sit watching ripples on the breeze-swathed water,
Leaves gently waving in the cool May wind.
Grey skies looming under crisp summer blue,
Thoughts of this world that nature struggles through.

We've done so much to our planet for greed,
Yet it continues to shape us with fire and ice.
Despite all the damage done to its might,
Mother Earth doesn't yield without the eternal fight.

Dazzle

Tuesday, 18 May 2021
12:58

Clouds float by my window, blinding white over dappled grey.
Crystal sapphire peeks through every now and then to scare
rain's blues away.

Sunshine makes me frown as the brightness dazzles my eyes,
Squinting to focus on what's around under beautifully
changing skies.

Cool breeze washes my face as a dull patch passes over,
Will it rain or stay quite dry? The skies look like they could
thunder.

Sun beats down again to clear the chill, stripping off those
layers,
Summer's here to dazzle again, in answer to nature's prayers.

Dark Dank Days in May

Friday, 21 May 2021
12:20

Dark skies perpetuate around the gloom-filled greys,
Dank as a cellar that long ago saw better days.

Dark swamps the mood from being constantly wet,
Dank to the core forces a grimace to those met.

Dark shapes grow darker with each twilight shower,
Dank soaking through til the brightest blooms cower.

Dark waters ripple with the ever-present rain,
Dank in May is life until our summer starts again.

Gold Dusk

Friday, 4 June 2021
03:03

Clouds hover low around the sun-kissed blue,
Creating colours in a forever-changing hue.

Golden rays burst from behind their veil,
Radiance so brilliant it seems never to fail.

Its richness gets deeper as the sun reclines,
A palette of yellows that deep turquoise defines.

Orange takes over whilst each minute does pass,
Peachy licks of fire under purple wisps amass.

As the sun continues under, its flames turn red,
Burnt orange flecked with every hue of yellow in your head.

Deeper and richer, painted with gold and musk,
Nature's wonder and its promise in this glorious dusk.

Clinging On

Monday, 14 June 2021
12:04

A Shrubs Point of View

Since my seed took hold, I've struggled and strived,
Through wind, hail, and snow, my shoots have survived.

Because I'm so small, my perch stays strong,
Just over the edge where the grass stays long.

My roots have gone deep to the water below,
Feeding on nutrients held within the steady flow.

The occasional bird nibbles at my leaves,
But I'm a little too high for most to perceive.

I can't stretch too far, for fear of the boats,
Watching the results when a passing branch floats.

I'm sticking to my spot, my sanctuary in the sun,
Where life is ok as long as I stay clinging on.

To Dance in the Wind

Wednesday, 30 June 2021
14:09

The grass is very high, my roots are so deep,
I'll take my chance to grow a few more feet.

This summer warmth has given me strength,
Plenty of rain, though the grounds not drenched.

My new shoots bristle, soaking in sun's light,
Giving me energy enough to beat any blight.

If I rise up enough as the cutters pass me by,
I'll get to dance in the wind before my leaves die.

Summer Rain

Monday, 5 July 2021
10:20

Grey doom flashed with blue fills a turbulent sky,
The sun can't peer through, no matter how hard it tries.
Winds are picking up, giving the leaves a shake,
The air takes on a chill before the heavens break.

The trees have damp sides from the previous showers,
Their roots almost throbbing with nature's great power.
As the drops start to fall, a shelter is welcomed,
The rustles of downpour as the torrents are opened.

Drops hit my head as I'm watching for a lull,
The damp mood deepens as the skies remain dull.
Heads hang low for those who just cannot wait,
The wet is less important than the chance of being late.

But then skies brighten, and the drops become small,
The sun appears once more as birds resume their call.
Pavements glisten as if with jewels from the sky,
Summer reappears, letting the spirits soar up high.

Orange Night

Sunday, 14 November 2021
22:17

After a warm autumn day,
The mist builds as cold dusk air creeps down from once clear
skies,

Thick haze blots out any definition of the universe,
Surrounding us living our winter lives.

As I peer out at the darkened glow,
The orange-hued sky hangs heavy all around,

Colours have disappeared into a night,
Lit by the city streets until morning is found.

The Orb

Thursday, 2 December 2021
22:17

My Favourite 'Chill Out' music.

Atmospheric sound,
Bass so profound.
A light refrain,
Depth builds again.
A voice speaks out,
Mechanicals shout.
Angels float down,
Harps and then clowns.
Meandering the mind,
Leaving sensation behind.
Divining through years,
The Orb dares you to hear.

Peace

I much prefer the occasional hoot of an owl to the squawking of geese,
Their incessant arguing seems to go in waves, never wanting to cease.
There's a calm on my boat, still in the night with nothing going to past,
My head full of thoughts, what's to do next, what did I do last?

The owl's stopped calling, a-hunting he goes, probably for a mouse,
The geese staying away, leaving the swans to tend to their house.
A ripple under the boat! Otters maybe or a bloody big fish,
Peace returns and my mind wanders towards tomorrow's relish.

Mellow

Friday, 22 April 2022
19:31

That sun-kissed feeling of warmth in your skin,
The headiness from drinking that grows within.
Sated with fine foods and sensational taste,
Relaxed in sound heaven, no desire for haste.

Is it really only April? The climate's so warm,
Forgetting the chill picks up after sun has gone.
Heading inside, the volume gets subdued,
Chilling on the sofa, my mind on more food.

I can't yet face trifle; there's still meat in my teeth,
The cushions get softer with bass shaking beneath.
I focus on my thoughts as the sky darkens to yellow,
Roll on the summer if it's going to be this mellow.

Sunset

Tuesday, 12 July 2022
20:07

Blue and white gold dazzles my eyes,
A few clouds build towards the west.
It's gonna be epic! Captivating skies,
The glory of Yorkshire's summer at its best.

Sipping and basking in intoxicating light,
This idyllic place fills my heart with joy.
Sun-kissed and relaxed on a fine July night,
So damn chilled even the midges don't annoy!

The gold gets richer each minute it subdues,
Our summer sun sinking into its bed of clouds.
Glowing fluffy white, changing gently its hues,
Covering brightness in their darkening shroud.

Gold turns to orange then plummets through red,
Clouds turning purple against a turquoise sky.
The sun hides behind its multicoloured bed,
Sinking into slumber as the day says goodbye.

Glow

Friday, 30 September 2022
20:51

My mind drifts into the hypnotic glow,
The arrow stove, its heat, a ceaseless flow.

Flickering flames wash over this scene,
Cosy and warm, the weather can't be seen.

I watch the dance of flame on wood and coal,
Yellows, orange, and reds warming my very soul.

Forgetting my pains that the cold dost blight,
My body sinking blissfully into an autumn night.

Public House

Monday, 10 October 2022
15:17

I hated pubs when growing up, smoky and drab and full of
old men in hats.
The smell of stale beer and cigarettes went home with me, the
stench would last.

Even in my late teens, I preferred getting smelly in the clubs
with music and dance.
A jukebox just didn't cut it and without dancing, getting
attached was just left to chance.

The smoking ban changed things and food suddenly became
a thing.
Craft ales started appearing and all of a sudden, my tastebuds
started to sing.

I quite often sit alone and soak in good flavours and vibes.
As I've got older, my retirement is happy with the sensations
a pub now provides.

Autumn Rain

It's been dry! So much so this year that I'm stuck on the canal,
There are worse places to be, I know, and I'm not yet facing
the banal.

If it was wet enough, I'd have to get moving every two weeks,
The regulations say I'm bound to a new tether I have to seek.

It's been raining all day! Damp dog and muddy wellies to boot,
The sound of raindrops pounding my roof has forced me to
take foot.

To the pub, we go. Getting rid of the crazy stir of being stuck
in one place,
I've got to like my local, the food, beers, and an amicable
space.

It's still too dry, I'm on my third pint and the peanuts have
created a thirst,
Darcy keeps finding new people to say hello to, for them, it's
his first.

It's pounding down outside, so I'm not going anywhere for a

while,
The pub menu is beckoning, a heartwarming meal to numb the home mile.

Locks

There's something quite soothing at night, listening to running water's constant low boil,
Only really audible when everything else goes quiet and you forget the day's woes and toil.

The by-wash gets loud when rain has fallen or boats are on the way downstream,
A low thundering roar drowns out most other sounds, waking the dog from his dreams.

As we walk by, Darcy always peers into the locks as if there might be something new,
I have to admit, I'm drawn to them as well, despite this being my daily view.

The top gates slightly open, released from a tight grip on the pressure that they trap,
The trickle of leaks where the debris of passing boats has got lodged, making gaps.

I hear metal clinking, telling me boats are heading up from the bottom gates,
Hopefully, they pass by quickly so I can continue with this life so sedate.

Chilled

There is a brilliance that only stopping and contemplating
what you see, feel, and hear can perceive,
I'm lucky, I get the opportunity to do that daily as I walk
Darcy, lie in my boat, listen to music, drink, taste, and believe.

People walk past Sophie, looking and wondering what boat
life must be like for someone living it on their own,
I see them pointing and chatting as I smile and reap the
rewards from long striving to plant these seeds I've sown.

The balance of my life is marked only by the sun's rise and
fall, setting out my routines to maximise being off-grid,
Condensation on windows seems to be my only real trial,
something I deal with openly rather than keeping hid.

Cleaning and maintaining Sophie is as easy as I want to make
it, taking minutes rather than hours in my daily life,
My retirement is therefore bliss, enjoying the finer things I can
afford, dreaming of pleasures, and forgetting strife.

Landlord

Timothy Taylor's Finest Yorkshire Ale

There's a mouthwatering anticipation when I know what's to
come,
That dark amber ale tempts my tastebuds like the sweetest
loam.

I watch it being poured as it swirls and froths in the glass,
My mind swirling with it as the settling and topping pass.

I pay with impatience as my lips desperately wait to sup,
Walking to a table holding that most precious of cups.

That first sip is sweetest as malt covers my tongue,
The bitter hops reminding me that I'm in my second home.

Ott

Listening to Ott's "Heads" Album for the Umptieth Time.

Oh, how this sound sends my mind in a spin,
Veering between deep pillars of bass and drum.

Each turn bringing new emotions from within,
Reaching the very heart with a beating thrum.

Tune after tune adding textures in my head,
Heavy with driving rhythm, then soft and light.

Expressing love for music's delicate threads,
Twisting and binding with electronic might.

Ott brings a skill that's been built from his past,
Producing inspiration from a sound that will last.

Fluff

Wednesday, 10 May 2023
22:07

New Cygnets on the Canal This Week

As I awake, her orange beak nudges me up,
Warm against my fluffy siblings, I struggle to stand.
We waddle with Mother to the water's sup,
Father catches the wind, making his feathers grand.

With beating wings, he shows us the way,
Gliding onto the water with beauty and grace.
Mother guiding us with her comforting sway,
We all keep together in such a hazardous space.

There's plenty to eat as the water is churned,
Paddling feet bringing up weeds from below.
We chirp with excitement as we twist and turn,
A breeze causing ripples, bouncing us to and fro.

Father dashes off; there's geese way upstream,
Beating his wings like thunder, scares them away.
Mother fluffs her feathers, showing how to preen,
We all keep in close, where it's safe to play.

Summer Sun

Sunday, 4 June 2023
15:33

Yet again it's scorching, my extremities are glowing,
Even with cooling winds, clouds are hardly showing.

It's too hot to be cooking, I've salad stuff a plenty,
Drinks are nicely chilled so my glass will not empty.

Content in my shady Cratch, watching people meander by,
The coolest amble in flowing white, anything darker I'd decry.

Music pumps out from my boat as I nod to those who smile,
With not a care in the world, I sip my drink, pondering for a
while.

Pain

There have been many instances where my thoughts bring out darker poetry. Writing them down and publishing the results has definitely helped me to deal with the pain felt at the time.

Drama

23 December 2015
12:23

Each day seems hard when inspiration wanes,
Adding to the workload with growing pains.
Chores seem tedious when there's no support,
Hindering the route that only order can sort.

Do I care that I've lost my drive?
Are my motives enough to survive?
Younger people seem to find the way,
Innovation used to be my shining day.

Alas, my creativeness has taken to flight,
Unable to reveal any power and might.
As I trudge on through without a goal,
Delivering me to a desert where nothing is whole.

Reading my thoughts, I glimpse my soul,
Adverse conditions creating a hole.
Maybe I'll snap out of it someday soon,
And start afresh with an inspired tune.

Numb

20 August 2016
23:17

Sitting too long on an economy plane,
Not even a stretch can diminish the pain.

Flights of fancy to a comfy bed,
Somewhere soft to rest a weary head.

My muscles ache with the urge to recline,
To close my eyes and free the mind.

Dreams of comfort beyond compare,
Maybe this journey will soon be there.

Tough

Tuesday, 21 March 2023
11:08

For my mum – Originally written in autumn 2014, two weeks before she died.

I know this is going to be tough,
My emotions in a stormy sea so rough, flow up and down like
a boat struggling to make ground.

I feel like I just want to cry,
Everything is so hard no matter how I try to manage the
situations that have caused so much emotional damage.

I ache with the strain of chores,
Driving an agenda that can't cure but will hopefully make life
a little more bearable and freer from strife.

I hope my efforts bear fruit,
My mum deserves the pursuit of happiness in the evening of
a life filled with sadness but also love and true meaning.

Home Late

Tuesday, 10 November 2020
21:56

I arrived home after three months of arduous cruising, several times over
The Pennines, on The Leeds/Liverpool, Bridgewater, Ashton, and
Rochdale canals; firstly, with my brother Nick, on what was meant to
be a three-week trip to Liverpool and back, and then mainly on my
own, with a few helpers along the route, getting stranded for two months
in Littleborough, above Manchester.
The story is on Facebook.

It's been hard, a trial of body, mind, hardiness, and
perseverance.
There've been times when I wished that turning left was not
the choice.
I've seen things, the like of which could make you weep or
dance.
My body cried with the pain of failing to hear common sense's
voice.

Sometimes it felt that all seemed to go against the flow.
Yet still I tried, fighting that urge to give in easily to fate.
Counting the days as time slowly edged to the day I could go.
Home again bound, grafting with new urgency to arrive so
late.

Thank you to Nick, Kate, Lily, Sam, and my saviour on several occasions, Dave.

Soul Searching

Tuesday, 17 November 2020
19:44

The warmth of today filled my heart with hope,
Sharing a walk, chatting, togetherness.
Country air-breathing life into my soul,
Heartfelt talk, rambling, inquisitiveness.

The warmth of that meeting filled my heart with hope,
Sharing experiences, reminiscing, thoughtfulness.
Walking together, though separated, felt so good,
Guiding my mind, sensations, closeness.

The cold in this evening made my heart go chill,
Wondering, searching, hopelessness.
Walking alone, dodging puddles, up that hill,
Exploring my soul for love's elusiveness.

The cold of these words bites my heart with a chill,
Protecting instinct starts to build its fortress.
Chilling night air bleeding hope from my soul,
Finding my relationship tree is, so far, fruitless.

Gander

Plagued night and day by their complaining squawk,
They belt out the cacophony as if warning of a hawk.
Waddling through the field, their clumsiness dismays,
Strutting like peacocks, they think they own the place.

The gaggle has grown, this year's brood have flourished,
With the gyms all closed, plenty of walkers, they're nourished.
Like gangs of youths, they cruise along the cut,
Necks extending, wings flapping, a waggle of butt.

Defending the towpath as if it's all their own,
Ruling the roost now the migration has flown.
Maybe the bravado is because they are scared,
Their might seems feeble against the mightiest bird.

With the power of a jet plane, daddy swan thuds in,
The geese all scatter as their cries go thin.
For a while, it's all quiet, the occasional flurry,
The world passes by, and no one seems in a hurry.

With signets safely passed, their parents glide away,
The geese have a gander, it's now safe to stay.
Peace returns with the occasional squawk,
then the noise increases, that bloody hawk.

Time

Saturday, 24 April 2021
04:41

Awake at 04:41!

My mind whirls at an unruly hour, keeping me awake,
Birds are singing before the rising sun.
My thoughts flash around stirring emotions for my heart's
sake,
Cold air keeps my body tightly spun.
My feet get too hot as time ticks away each dawning hour,
Tingles make my skin twitch and burn.
My eyes ache as they wearily focus on my brain's power,
Joints and muscles tell me it's time to turn.

Hush

Wednesday, 12 May 2021
22:06

Something I said made you go quiet,
My heart aches for love's amorous riot.

Can it be repaired or is it too late,
Will my soul be condemned to this fate?

My mind races with questions and doubts,
This yearning for answers I hesitate to shout.

Will you be here to soothe my woes?
Have I said too much? Is this how it goes?

Something I said has battled your mind,
My heart aches for love left behind.

My Little Girl

My little girl's lost, her confidence is shot.
Lockdown's salvo is burning red hot.

Her friends are so far from the place she is at.
They seem to be coping with life's this and that.

How can I help her? She fights with herself.
Much longer off school will leave her on a shelf.

The counsellor says one thing, support officer another.
But would it solve anything if they all worked together?

Her heart is breaking the spirit that was abound.
Hopefully, my confident little girl's soul can be found.

May My Heart Stay Calm.

Monday, 31 May 2021
20:09

A hole has appeared, the emptiness aches.
Where once dwelt a deep love, lies only waste.

It was full for a while, my soul flew up high,
The rollercoaster of pleasure soaring through sky.

That lightning bolt had struck, it felt so real.
My heart was on my sleeve showing how I feel.

Was it too much for a tired soul to bear?
The intensity of my passion can attract and scare.

What I had to offer was obviously too much,
Maybe the next one will likewise care such.

My search continues to find love's great balm.
My soul remains strong, may my heart stay calm.

Shame

Sunday, 20 June 2021
21:25

I was transfixed by that smile,
Lips so full of a promise.

Eyes of blue-green like emeralds,
I'd fall into them as I kiss.

Skin so fair as the spring,
Glowing with the promise of life.

What beauty is found so nearby,
It's a shame there's no love in sight.

Hung

Sunday, 10 April 2022
14:43

My mind numbed with the wool of an imbibe or two,
Slightly nauseous when horizontal and staying near the loo.
"Never again" has been uttered several times before,
At least I stayed upright, not left hugging the floor.

"'Twas and amusing night" as memories flood back,
The telling of stories and laughing at the crack.
One too many or was it one for the road?
It matters not now the camel's back has been rode.

Bacon sarnies and coffee started to work their magic,
Settling the churn that through the night had been tragic.
The thought of a drink very far from my mind,
Until 'Hair of the dog' Carling reminds me that I have some
wine!

B.O.A.T.

This Is a Long Gripe!

I was going to start with "All the best things in life are free"?
Oh yeah, somebody's already written that so let's see.
I bought my boat Sophie to live a nice life quite cheaply,
However, **Bring Out Another Thousand** hits the pockets deeply.
First, it was the gearbox that unwound all of its screws,
That was only fifty quid; Ian from Pennine saved me worse news.
The calorifier came next leaking foul smelly water,
It had been fixed before but not as it ought to.
With too much pressure the fracture reappeared,
So a new tank and expansion had to be commandeered.
Five hundred and fifty quid but I fitted it on my own,
Eating into my contingency money so I didn't need a loan.
The solar was a bargain and it's paid back already,
My boat was energy efficient as long as I took it steady.
Unfortunately, whilst off cruising, into the Pennines we travelled,
My brother Nick's ill-placed weed hatch was when it next unravelled.

Sophie's engine was drowned, the bedroom an inch under,
Another few minutes and our trip would have come asunder.
Fortunately for us, I think clearly under such stress,
It didn't take long to bail out and dry up the damp mess.
Nick offered to pay; a new Beta Marine could be grave,
But the engine was revived by my new best mate Dave.
We carried on our trip until the prop coupling came off,
Dave to the rescue again? Absolutely I say, he's my hero, don't scoff.
A new aluminium block later, another five hundred quid,
Surely this must be the end of it, any more surprises been hid?
All seemed to be going well and we'd get to Liverpool Dock,
Then my luck ran out as third time unlucky, I fell in the lock!
Fortunately, I didn't panic, "Nick quickly shut the gate paddle!"
After losing my glasses and pride, I dried off and got back on the saddle.
Cruising with new gusto, I obviously wasn't full of attention,
My new hood hit a footbridge causing more consternation.
I could still get it up fortunately as the late summer rain dropped,
And things seemed to run smoothly for a while until everything stopped.
The canal was shut due to a leak and meant all the water had gone,
But never mind, I'm in my boat! Wherever I moor up is my home.
I settled in for the autumn, it'd be six weeks until the leak's fixed,
Then my batteries started playing nasty "running out of power" tricks.

I bit the bullet and bought a new set of high-performance AGMs,
Another five hundred quid bought slightly earlier than I expected them.
I survived the rest of the autumn without any further cost,
And I crossed all my fingers that I'd return before all was lost.
After finally getting home again, before Christmas I might add!
I totted up the price of living cheaply and extra expenses I'd had.
I've spent about ten grand in the two years on my lovely boat,
Despite two drownings, the engine still works and I'm happily afloat.
As the cost-of-living rockets, life on board has more appeal,
My boat's increased in value so even with what I've spent, it's still a steal!

Sheep

Saturday, 17 December 2022
03:58

It's four in the morning and I'm wide awake,
I've tried closing my eyes, almost counting sheep.
If only my mind would stop, for goodness's sake,
The fire's stoked, it's warm, I just need sleep.

I keep thinking about love, maybe one day to share,
A mermaid or an angel to nurture my heart.
Pretty as a picture with Flaming June's red hair,
Blue eyes that dazzle even when so far apart.

Counting continues as I play a quick game,
Trying to take my mind off my soul's desire.
My eyes grow weary as concentration wanes,
Closing my eyes, the sheep count transpires.

As the fog descends over my train of thought,
That pretty face remains at the front of mind.
I hope we hook up and find a feeling of sorts,
Something's quite special about this "one of a kind".

Creaking & Swaying

Sunday, 29 January 2023
16:13

Sophie moves back and forth under a constant wind,
Ropes stretching tight under the stress of weather's battle.

She creaks when strong gusts blow up from behind,
Rocking and swaying, making all the loose things rattle.

Rain beats on my windows as the gale blows its top,
Trying its best to dampen spirits with the boiling gloom.

But my fire's warm and I'm cosy until the torrent does stop,
Sophie keeps me protected in her safe steel cocoon.

Block

Tuesday, 28 March 2023
13:47

Twiddling my thumbs whilst it rains outside my boat.

I want to write something, but I can't think what,
My head's so full of emotion, I have writer's block.
Fleeting words and flashing thoughts keep passing me by,
But sentences elude me and I'm really not sure why.

Poetry is spontaneous for me, and it's never really planned,
I think of a situation or feeling, and words easily spring to
hand.
Thinking 'I must write a poem' isn't really my thing,
Similar to when I used to write songs for my band to sing.

So 'come on brain' let's write something inspired by the time,
A word or two to express how the oysters of the world are
mine.
Some ditties or a dirge, letting everyone know how I feel,
Just easy to read when there's a few moments to steal.

Something

Wednesday, 10 May 2023
14:41

There are thoughts in my head, both good and bad,
I just can't seem to grasp anything happy or sad.
David Bowie once said "If I'm settled, I can't write",
Maybe that's what's giving me this creative blight.

My heart is settled, there's no more striving for love,
That yearning is fulfilled by my angel from above.
Sophie is doing nicely, nothing stressful has gone wrong,
I'm living an easy life, building romance, having fun.

Passion

This set of poems started after buying my boat, Sophie, changing my life, and waiting to get on board, which then led to the start of finding new love. Because of the nature of my thoughts, some old poems re-surfaced during this time and in some cases were rewritten. The published poems are all featured in themed anthologies of various poets.

The Time for New Life

03 January 2020
11:59

I can't wait,
Meals on my plate count off one by one at a pace so slow,
The time gone seems as endless as the time to come.

I contemplate,
Such peace I will feel in my own space afloat at a pace so slow,
The time to spend doing things with those I love and time alone.

I anticipate,
Hard times ahead as motions of change take hold before beginning to slow,
The time now preparing for what's to come will make a good job done.

I hesitate,
Shocks to the system of life can affect heart and mind adjusting to a pace so slow,
The time taken to handle this well must bear fruit to sweeten what's to come.

I must wait,

Moving too fast now will overturn the efforts and thought put into a pace too slow,
The time given to waiting for the right moment enables challenges to be overcome.

It's never too late,
New life will inspire me to take on new challenges and enjoy the pace so slow,
The time and experience of renewing my lust for life will be second to none.

Friend

This singleton life is ok whilst my dream unfolds, but what then?
There are times that need experiences to be shared, but who with?

It's been forever since intimacy was a part of my life, but how long?
My heart tells me that my mind needs to be released, but why now?

The condition of my life has found its place, but where next?
Can a special friend share in the joys that I yearn for, but what way?

Blue Sky

Eyes shine with the hazy blue of a summer afternoon sky,
Intense with a passion and expression to fill the mind and
soul.

Flowing hair framing a beauty found rarely but often seen,
Delicate curls drifting without effort over the glowing skin.

A smile wrought from experience finessed by lines of a
healthy life,
Lips full of promise that a giving heart would melt at their
touch.

Cheeks so defined and soft to embrace in a beautiful caress,
To hold that face in my mind would be pure satisfaction as I
kiss.

SB (Someone Beautiful)

Monday, 23 November 2020
16:31

Simplicity is a true sign of unfettered beauty,
Based on purity as the eye beholds.

Sensuality drawn from the corners of lips,
Breathing new life into an idealism so old.

Serenity finds depth in dark shining eyes,
Beneath the surface, passion burns out the cold.

Spectacularly pretty to one who feels love,
Breaking away from that predictable mould.

Glint

There's a sparkle in those eyes that draws me in close when I gaze,
With that effortless smile, natural happiness sets my heart ablaze.
Shining bright, the reflections dazzle like a million stars,
Such beauty fills my mind with a galaxy of dreams so far.

There's a glint in those eyes that turns any chill with a burning fire,
Bursting my heart with so many explosions of pure desire.
Shining bright, that gaze calms and soothes the harshest woes,
Love flows from within, through such beauty, to those she beholds.

There's a love in those eyes that cares for all in her grasp,
Empathy pouring around, cushioning from the emotional blasts.
Shining bright like a beacon to draw you to the safety of home,
This beauty clears a clouded heart of any fear about what's to come.

The Lovers

Monday, 30 November 2020
13:51

First written in 1999. Published 2006 by Forward Press Ltd. Re-edited 30/11/2020.

A whisper, a giggle, a broad knowing grin,
Longing enhanced by the pictures within.
Smooth like cream, a delicate button,
Touched so softly like silk or fine cotton.

Beautiful curves brightly tingling with life,
Yielding to caress so tender and light.
Warmth so strong, lips melt with bliss,
Drawing ever closer with lingering kiss.

Fantasy exploding emotions and lust,
Sweetly enshrouded with bonds of deep trust.
Aquiver with delight, passions ablaze,
Exciting sensations that constantly amaze.

Wet lips touch, pressed firmly with love,
Embraced in skin softer than clouds above.
Soaring with pleasure, sensations, and touch,
Ascending to an ecstasy that bears so much.

Fulfilled beyond dreams with a kiss so pure,
Gasping, heart pounding, left wanting for more.
Softness pressed together, enveloped in rest,
Drifting into thoughts of the other at best.

A whisper, a giggle, a broad knowing grin,
Bringing love ever closer, beginning again.

Ecstasy

Saturday, 5 December 2020
13:39

Written in 1999 Published by Forward Press 2006

Soft, warm, glowing bright,
Sensuality so dear.
Heavenly pleasure, sheer delight,
Holding you so near.

Soft, warm flowing curves,
Delightfully sublime.
Heaving, arching, tingling nerves,
Intoxication divine.

Soft, warm drifting clouds,
Surround you in desire.
Deep, strong beating heart,
Stoked with passion's fire.

Soft, warm, sating bliss,
Enveloped in tender love.
Carried off in fantasy,
To a sanctuary far off.

After All This Time

This feeling I've found in my heart seems different from those
few times before,
Maybe my soul's experiences have taught me something this
strong means so much more.

My heart wants to sing out with the passion that was felt with
the kiss, caress, and lust,
The aching deep inside is surely sign of something within
which I can put my soul's trust.

To feel this good was something my heart could only dream
in fantasy to fulfil,
My soul seems calmed by the knowledge that only a mutual
understanding can instil.

My heart beats with a rhythm matched by the fire that I felt,
oh so deep inside,
Throwing caution to the wind my soul expresses a desire that
I don't want to hide.

Perfect

Tuesday, 15 December 2020
06:51

Lines of health and life create perfect dimples around your lips,

Full and soft, perfect lips draw me into your gentle fingertips.

Finely painted, perfect slender fingers entrap me between your thighs,

Toned and soft, your perfect thighs wrap around my wanton sighs.

With a smooth softness, your perfect skin succumbs to my gentle touch,

Kissing with passion, your perfect body envelops me as you give so much.

Shits 'n' Giggles

My body aches now in the most pleasant way,
I've giggled like a child enjoying exciting play.
Something so eloquently written made me cry,
Words fill my heart whilst the smile never dies.

What an incredible mind, full of humour and wit,
Strong with life's experiences, taking no shit.
Smiling through it all with an inimitable shine,
Fuelled by a desire and plenty of red wine.

Tale after tale speaks of family love and strife,
Trouble at the supermarket, the traumas of life.
Middle-age spread, going grey in your prime,
Trying to be cautious but enjoying a good time.

One thing is certain in my mind after one day,
There's a place in my heart where someone will stay.
Kisses and cuddles will be rewarded with love,
Shits 'n' giggles! ooh eck! Ey up! Heavens above!

My Love I Feel

Friday, 30 April 2021
07:50

My head is filled with you,
My soul is refreshed by you,
My mind is on fire in your glow,
My heart refuses to slow,
My face lights up when you ping,
My whole body just wants to sing,
My emotions are running so wild,
I feel like an excited child.

Wild Beasts

Sunday, 2 May 2021
21:50

You make me feel very special today,
My heart melts with each thing you say.
Your eyes tell me so much that I cry,
Tears filled with elation, too much to dry.

As they run down my cheeks, your words soothe,
Deep emotions flow as your fingers move.
My skin is alive at the tenderness of your touch,
Skipping and shaking, my body feels so much.

You hold my cheek, and your eyes fill with love,
Happiness pouring out as if released from way above.
Your smile lights my soul so deep I can feel,
The racing of your pulse as my mind reels.

I tell you how I feel, and the sparkle ignites,
Flutters and aching so impossible to fight.
Passion takes hold deep in my thighs,
Breathing is heavy as love's flames soar so high.

May Day

Monday, 3 May 2021
13:06

I close my eyes and hold your glowing face in my hands,
Pull you to my breast and envelope you in my strength.

I can feel the beating of your heart slowing down,
As you sink into my embrace of understanding and loam.

My mind races with the pain you have shared,
How can I help this light in my life stay so bright?

I squeeze you tightly as our bodies enfold,
Your head on my chest as I breathe out your woes.

I stroke your hair as I whisper my love,
Feeling you closer as I soothe and caress.

You raise your eyes to meet mine with sweet grace,
As we travel together to our heavenly place.

Smitten

Tuesday, 4 May 2021
20:09

I dream of a life not yet complete,
The battles of love I've yet to defeat.
Such times when I pause you fill my mind,
Searching for perfection I'm about to find.

Not a moment goes by without your beaming smiles,
Creating such love that could span everlasting miles.
Can this be true, my heart is truly taken at last?
My yearning for you near filling my loving repast.

I ache for your touch, my mind races so fast,
Pounding a rhythm that my passion has cast.
Waiting for your call, a text, and our chat,
I've fallen for you, it's as simple as that.

I've loved this quick journey to find your heart,
Realising how special you are from the start.
Now that I've caught your attention with mine,
I'm ready for a romance, deep, intense, and divine.

The Mountain Top

There's no way I'm hiding how I feel,
My heart aches with emotions and thrills.
This body floats as if the ground isn't real,
I'm intoxicated beyond any trip from pills.

Someone has pulled me to their heart,
My thoughts are filled with their loam.
This soul was enriched from the start,
Singing from the heavens where love roams.

I want to shout out from on high,
My life has been missing such bliss.
This could be the love of my life,
Every moment together with her I miss.

I should keep my feelings in check,
My caution when expressing my deep love.
This moment is unique so what the heck!
An angel has swooped to save me from above.

Bowled

Friday, 7 May 2021
19:29

I try to walk under the intoxication of your lust,
My mind whirling in a dream I'm grasping to trust.

A fire inside me blazes around your incredible touch,
My loins ache with a passion that was almost too much.

The depth of your kiss held me in a trance,
My heart gave in, seduced in such erotic dance.

You held my eyes with the intensity of your gaze,
I'm bowled over with how you've set my soul ablaze.

Lips on My Glass

Saturday, 8 May 2021
10:43

You sipped my wine as you gazed into my eyes,
We talked through our past and how it affected our lives.

Your mouth I could kiss, every moment you spoke,
Our conversation! Oh wow! Such emotions it evoked.

You shone with a halo so bright I could faint,
This picture in my mind better than any I could paint.

My heart is aching for our next meeting to pass,
Until then I'm reminded by your lips on my glass.

A Recipe for Love?

Sunday, 9 May 2021
00:51

Two souls seeking truth,
One common thought or ideal.
Two hearts that struggled through youth,
One goal for two minds to feel.
Two seconds to find that spark,
One night to reflect and yearn.
Two minds that seem to be one,
One word that comes easily to both.
Two journeys have ended with love,
One passion soaring so high above.

Apart

Monday, 10 May 2021
15:35

My heart aches when my body longs for you to be here,
With my mind creating the senses and scents when you are
near.

I feel my blood filling me to the highest crest,
As with love my whole hears and sees the rising of your chest.

My head flows with the pleasures of your love,
And your breath takes me higher than anything above.

I move my hands over the soft thoughts of your skin,
To carry you, my love, as a picture I hold within.

When we're apart my healed soul eases the strain,
My heart and mind shorten time til you're here again.

That Smile

Friday, 25 June 2021
00:45

I smiled as you reached out to me again,
My soul was reminded of your sweet face.
My heart skipped a beat now and then,
As we discussed a meeting time and place.

My mind wandered into your eyes,
That smile drawing me into your charms.
I'm so glad we never said our goodbyes,
My thoughts drift in between your soft arms.

I'm thrilled that you want us to meet,
My soul needs the healing of you near.
That smile will shine like the sun's heat,
I know you'll find nothing in me to fear.

My heart is beating with new blood,
The excitement of meeting you at last.
I know this will do us both good,
Maybe help us to block out our past.

Your Heart, My Love

Tuesday, 13 July 2021
03:31

Your touch fills my heart with such joy,
I float on the feathers of your fingertips.
My smile beams like a child with a new toy,
I drift into the curves of your sweet lips.

Your eyes glow with a passion that I adore,
I'm engulfed in the green pools of their gaze.
My heart beats like a hammer in the forge,
I'm entranced by that fire I see ablaze.

Your face lights up when you catch my glance,
I feel your love touch deep inside my heart.
My body skips a beat as my soul's romanced,
I hold you close even when we're left apart.

Your voice takes my mind through your soul,
I'm smitten with the tones and your laugh.
My happiness when with you makes me whole,
I'm in love with you as we share our new path.

Hugs

As I look into your eyes you wrap your arms around my shoulders and pull me into you,
My cheek brushes your hair as I wrap around your waist and squeeze tightly.

I hear you breath in as your heart beats against my chest and we become one,
I feel your lips on my neck in a wanton kiss delivered ever so lightly.

Our love leaves us spent in each other's arms as you lie on my chest stroking soft hairs,
I kiss your head as you sink deeper into my embrace, our hearts beating together.

As I talk about my life, you gently giggle and squeeze me whilst I picture your smile,
Hugging you leaves sensations so addictive that I want them to last forever.

Whirring

The cogs of my mind are spinning in tune to my boat waking.
The engine of my heart whirring as my mind dreams of lovemaking.
My head spins with the intoxication of love into which I'm falling.
There is no beginning, no middle, no end to the sensations overtaking and enthralling,
Your face lights up in my memories of our bodies embracing.
Your glow fills my thoughts as each touch and caress keeps my heart racing.
Our breath becomes one in my mind in passion with each kiss I'm facing.
Our hearts whirring on as each moment builds pictures never erasing.

My Heart This Feels

Monday, 19 July 2021
13:20

My heart is with someone I can't be with all the time, but I don't mind.
This soul has been joined by a radiance so bright it has left me blind.

My body aches for a touch so deep that my senses are alive.
This incredible angel has lifted me up from a long search where I strive.

My yearning drives a passion that doesn't know how to hold back.
This feels like the part of me experiencing what my previous lives lack.

Infinitely Awake

Monday, 19 July 2021
13:21

As my mind races and my heart pounds,
The constant adrenaline of this emotional barrage of my soul
keeps me.

Awake, despite my tiredness,
Alert despite my head being in the clouds.
Aware of you in my depths,
Around you with my embrace.
Awestruck by your beauty,
Astounded by your thoughts.
Attuned to your psyche,
Accepting your sweet words.
All giving of my heart,
At the height of my love.

A Passion So Divine

Monday, 19 July 2021
13:22

I lie spent in your arms,
My body drenched in your love.
I succumbed to your charms,
My soul soared high above.
Clouds disappeared,
Your sunshine glowed bright.
Our passion heard,
Throughout this wonderful night.
Our bodies entwined,
Your mind bound to mine.
Our love redefined,
In a passion so divine.

That's How It Works!

Monday, 5 December 2022
23:46

There are real-life beautifully adorned mermaids in this world,
I've known a few, shining like stars but too distant to be
adored.

I met one today from across the hills whose brilliance shone
so bright,
Drawing me into her waters where my heart might swim
without plight.

Her honesty, so clear, filled my soul with a wanton throbbing
ache,
And she showed me her life, sharing those she loves with
refreshing faith.

I've seen her ass! We've not yet met but her body art has sent
me berserk,
I like what I see, I don't want to "fuck off", I know that's how
it works.

Angelic

It seems a vision has descended from on high and taken hold
of my heart,
Her wings beautifully spread and wrapping me gently in her
golden glow.

A smile that shines with a brightness that captivated my gaze,
Kindness that can only come from the sweetest and purest of
souls.

My angel, sweeping me off my life-wearied feet and carrying
me aloft,
One kiss, all I needed to know that something between us has
clicked.

Our hands entwined, as if they'd always known how that
touch would feel,
I can't wait to find out how many "perfect partner" boxes
have been ticked.

Getting Me

Friday, 17 March 2023
11:30

To find someone who understands me is a wonderful thing,
Sharing emotions, on to which our wounded hearts cling.

Taking the time to work out what makes this someone tick,
Getting to know them slowly, not falling for the old tricks.

Sharing our lives in detail and not holding anything back,
Beginning something new and special without running off
track.

Getting me has meant that I've discovered my new drive,
I'm happy to have found someone with whom love can thrive.

My Heart

Monday, 10 July 2023
13:13

It's been a challenging few years, searching my soul,
Trying to find true love and make my life whole.

I've made mistakes, the road sometimes so rough,
I'd a feeling, after so long, that this would be tough.

There's been times when I gave up on finding that one,
With so many failures and my spirit had almost gone.

Settling for "not quite right" gave my heart respite,
But before too long, caused that internalising fight.

Then completely by chance, I met an open heart,
Pretty as a peach, we got on well from the start.

And despite a near miss when I thought all was lost,
My heart has been sated and true love has no cost.

There will be more poems, no doubt.
Tim

Other Musings

ORBS

18 October 2019
20:57

I remember cold, wet misery waiting for my bus in the middle of winter on Saturday afternoon with heavy bags to carry home when I got off at a stop too far away to be convenient.

The red brick building was dingy and always milling with dirty dishevelled shoppers, bags full of bargains from the plethora of cheap shops at that end of town; depressing is too short a description.

Thankfully, the Old Red Bus Station is now a warm music-filled haven from the cold and wet autumn weather, conveniently near the car park I use for my Mercedes Benz.

How times have changed as I think back whilst enjoying a drink amongst the warm hubbub of Friday nighters, chatting about their week and how they'd like to unwind.

The bass from the next room drowns out any definition in the background music; things will be very different later when the DJs start spinning their magic and the tunes start banging.

But none of this matters at the moment as I marvel at what a great job the new owners have done to create an inspiring, fun, cultural experience out of something that was about to be demolished.

A building with such menial history doesn't normally survive the ambitions of developers to create new attractions for wealth but I'm pleased to hear the ORBS is here to stay for now.

Cheers!

Gothic

Whitby Goth Weekend Saturday - What a day!

Well, after gothing it up with makeup and painted nails, my mask, hat, and leathers, spending the day in Whitby on Sunday with my beautiful lady was an absolute pleasure.

Whilst the rain poured down, we browsed and shopped in the Goth Markets at The Leisure Centre and then the Pavilion. Several brooches, a ring, and a rather nice cane later we met up with the gang, and then the sun came out to invite us round Whitby with the most fantastically bright and clear double rainbow.

The first stop was The Great Goth Shop to cure my Boot Envy. Sporting a newly purchased pair of incredible New Rock boots, I then tried walking in a straight line without crashing into anything/anyone; very difficult when admiring the boots, I'd just bought! I felt like I did when I got my first pair of red wellies. I couldn't take them off.

We met up with more of the gang at The Whitby Museum Gardens for a hilarious photo shoot involving slipping photographers, several tries at a location, blood-sucking antics, and some seriously good posing.

Another market inside an old church gave a spectacular setting and inspired Terri to buy me a most fabulous purple waistcoat which of course I had to wear straight away, strutting even more in my ridiculously chunky heeled boots.

All of a sudden, we only had an hour before the shops shut so I had to walk quickly (without looking at my boots) which demonstrated how 'so goddamn comfy' New Rocks are! Fortunately, we made it quickly to the shopping streets, which was a good job.

The place was packed with onlookers, shoppers, photographers, admirers, and fellow Goths, all vying for the few feet of street available. Some great sights, decorations, and particularly gorgeous outfits to behold and we got stopped several times to pose for pictures. And apparently, this was quiet compared to the previous day!

A couple of final photo opportunities arose as we headed across the harbour bridge for a hike back up the hill to our car. The spring in my step never faltered until I sat in my car trying to get my legs under the steering wheel! It's impossible to drive a Mercedes A-Class in New Rock boots! Quick change back into my trainers as the sunset and the clouds went from vanilla, through orange and red to grey.

Silence

Thursday, 10 November 2022
22:33

The is no real silence, unless profoundly deaf. The quiet can be taken for silence by many people, but there's always noise, whether around you or in the mind bank of things your ears have experienced, and brain recognises. The imagined world around us can be as real and as noisy as life.

Even for the deaf, noise at certain levels can be perceived. The depth of bass is felt as clearly as heard when at the right level. I've only, however, experienced partial deafness when my ears have been so clogged with wax and infection that the only noise I perceive is tinnitus. Those who help deaf people experience music are to be greatly admired.

When you tune your ears to the quiet, the sounds you pick up become infinitely complex and innumerable. There are definite recognised sounds but beyond that, there are a myriad of noises that start to become apparent the more you concentrate on the quiet and start filtering out the recognised sounds.

Most of this is mingled into "the boil" as I call it, be it traffic or water; the sound of quietly boiling water and burning gas.

White noise, how it's also referred to, tends to mask the finer sounds for most people, and their natural noise filters prevent them from really experiencing how noisy silence actually is.

Despite the fact that I listen to a lot of very loud music, the enigma that I can hear as well as I do leaves me understanding that I'm lucky, I know; I'd hate to be permanently or profoundly deaf.

To live without sound and particularly music is something I hope I never have to experience.

Silence is, however, something to also be enjoyed, despite how noisy it is.

Man's Best Friend

Darcy amuses me with his little routines in our daily life aboard Sophie. He has different routines at the house (I know he prefers it there) and I'm intrigued as to how his mind works in each environment.

I regularly find him sprawled out on the sofa bed near the warm stove during the night. If I find him curled up tightly then I know the boat has got too cold. I put a blanket over him, for which he sighs deeply, then stoke the fire to get it going again. He sighs again as I stroke his head before returning to bed. He never sleeps on my bed but always sleeps on a bed at the house, either Kate's or her mum's.

When I get up in the morning, he doesn't move as I go about my routine of putting the kettle on, sorting the dried pots and pans, etc from the previous night's washing up, making a cuppa, and then checking the windows and sorting out any condensation as my tea brews.

He waits until he hears me get out of the shower before getting up and stretching, sometimes with a noisy yawn, and then comes to see if I'm getting ready to go for a walk. He always looks at me as if to say, "Hurry up Dad, need a wee!" And then ambles back to his bed or the sofa.

He comes back after I've brushed my teeth and squeegeed the shower screen, obviously sounds he's listening out for again, then watches me get dressed, tail wagging as he recognises walking clothes, whilst excitedly walking back and forth from bedroom to main room.

He generally stands near where I keep his collar looking at the door and then at me as I don my coat, hat, etc., and then once his collars on, stands in the way of the door so I have to get him to move before I put my boots on.

He waits until I command him to actually go out, and he usually checks through the Cratch cover windows and often growls if he sees something/someone nearby. He sheepishly looks at me straight after a growl as if apologising and sometimes sits down without me telling him to be quiet.

If he's been good and not growled, he gets to go straight out before me, otherwise, I make him wait until I'm out before saying, "C'mon then."
As all dogs do, Darcy goes straight for the nearest lamppost to check out the news and cock his leg, then checks out every lamppost, shrub, tuft of grass, or molehill along our route.

He always waits until he finds a suitably grassy patch before doing his business. I tried to train him to go near bins, but it's the grass that's important to him. He will then spend the rest of the walk sniffing or finding sticks and becoming a puppy again as he playfights with them excitedly, looking at me to see if I approve or will join in.

He always looks at me after any interaction with other dogs or humans, as if he's checking that it's ok to do that. If he gets spooked and his hackles go up, he will look at me with his tail between his legs because he knows he's being naughty, particularly if he growls. He'll then trot off with his ears back and tail still between his legs, regularly looking back, if I've had to be stern with him. His gait changes as soon as he hears a "good boy".

I very rarely have him on a lead because he's so well-behaved. If we're visiting somewhere new or walking along main roads, I tether him but otherwise, he's a free agent as long as he's near and not eating stuff or rolling in anything; for which he gets an "Hoi!" or "Off!". I spent many hours training him to respond to my voice and hand gestures and he instantly changes his behaviour.

His recall is excellent because I practice it regularly and although not brilliant, he will walk at heel when asked and constantly reminded.
I spent a lot of time training him about safe pavement and dangerous road so I could keep him off the lead as much as possible. He doesn't get that cars, etc. are dangerous but he does automatically stop at any road crossing and unless goaded by someone he knows, never crosses a road unless I say its ok to, with "go on then", to which he always runs straight across.

When we're walking along the towpath, he'll invariably stop right in front of pedestrians and cyclists who have to veer around or brake as he nonchalantly looks at me and then at them.

He seeks out attention from anyone he likes the look of and will get giddy if they reciprocate with strokes and cuddles. He's always different and very gentle with small children but gets very involved with adults, particularly if female.

Ball is of course his favourite pastime as with most dogs. He'll carry his ball all the way to the playing field, run around like a nutter catching it before it stops bouncing, and then carry the ball most of the way back until his jaws are obviously aching (he puts the ball down gently, licking his lips and then stretches his jaws in a big yawn) when I to pick it up. He'll always expect the ball back however if we cross a road!

After a walk, he will expectantly wait for a biscuit or chew stick depending on the time of day, and then settle down to snooze in his bed as I go about my boat. He'll only look up if he thinks there's food that he might get a taste of. The pate wrapper, an end of Polish sausage, fat of the bacon, spare rib bones are just some of his favourites.

When Darcy's at the house, he'll jump onto a chair or bed, without asking permission, any time he feels like it. On the boat, however, he won't get up until encouraged by me or whoever's on board, whether it's occupied or not. As soon as I leave the sofa at night to go to bed, however, he's straight on it, bagging the warm spot. I vacuum the sofa daily due to my boy's incessant malting.

His funniest routine, and something I miss when he's not with me, is the 'playtime' after I've washed the cafetière and filled it with a bit of hot water to warm it, something I do almost every morning. As soon as he hears the plunger drop, he's up and looking for a toy to bring me for a quick game of fetch or tug of war. Lots of giddy growling and tail wagging ensues for the next few minutes until I get up and make my coffee.

I always smile very fondly whilst making my morning coffee, whether he's there or not.

As you no doubt have gathered, I love my dog.

Music Makes Everything OK

I remember my son's birth reasonably well, but the traumatic things stick in my mind most of all. His mum was rushed into hospital four weeks before the due date, suffering from acute Pre-Eclampsia. She had to be immediately induced before I'd got there. She was drowsy with drugs and in the delivery suite when I arrived, and I nearly passed out when they gave her an epidural and her waters broke.

I don't remember much more about Sebastian's birth apart from cutting the umbilical cord and then holding him whilst they stitched his mum up. He opened his eyes as I was showing him the world, in what I can only describe as a "Delboy moment" when Damian was born in "Only Fools and Horses".

The love I felt for him was epic.
He then spent seven days in an incubator because he'd been premature, had the umbilical cord wrapped round his neck during birth, and acquired jaundice; quite common in premature babies, so I was told. Watching him and only being able to stroke him was heart-wrenching for his mum, and I but we soon had him home and he filled our lives with joy,

laughter, and love.

Kate was born by appointment in the BRI maternity suite operating theatre, with much planning several weeks beforehand. She was breached and therefore could only be delivered via caesarean section at eight-thirty a.m. on 25/06/2008

Her mum and I chose some music to play in the operating theatre which ended up being our favourite CD from Ibiza; The Chillout Session.
I can only remember nice things from that birth and usually, when I hear one or more of the tracks that played for that forty-five minutes we were in the room with the doctors and nurses, who all seemed to be enjoying the vibe.
I had that "Delboy Moment" with Kate too, but the main thing I remember was enjoying it.

T R Phillips - Proud father of two music lovers.

Just One Thing

If I was only allowed to have one thing in life, what would it be?

The answer is easy, but it makes me think about what is really important in my life.

I remember when that one thing was a toy, or my dog Goldie, my favourite bike that I thought I'd broken when I got it for Christmas, only to find when I'd stopped crying that my mum had fixed it, just like that!

When in my teens/twenties, the one thing I wanted was not to make the same mistakes my parents did. So much for that one as far as my marriages are concerned!

When my son was born, growing up, and becoming a man, I vowed to ensure that I was part of his life as much as he wanted me to be. For that, like any parent must feel, I am truly grateful, and very much thankful that his mum and I worked very hard to make it that way when we divorced.

Now I'm watching my daughter grow and start to deal with

teenage life and her parents living separate lives, I'm very conscious of how carefully I need to tread in order to keep her safe and happy. Kate brought that sunshine back into my life when she was born and I've tried to make the most of my time with her as she's grown, loving our play together, feeling her love as she cuddles me, and how secure she felt in my hands when little.

Despite all I've been through, the pain and hardship I've endured, I still feel very lucky with the life I've had because of Seb and Kate. Their love for me makes it all worthwhile; I know that what they've experienced will help them in their relationships and in bringing up my grandchildren when that eventually happens.

When I found my dog, Mr Darcy, and rescued him from an uncertain future in Cyprus, I started to truly see how much you get from what you give. His behaviour, obedience, attention, and playfulness are driven by one thing, love; if he's feeling loved, he knows he's been good, and he gets fed/a treat/his ball/a walk in the woods to find sticks and splash in the stream.

So, the simplicity of that one thing I want is clear because of the results of what I've put into attaining it so far.

I'm sure you may have guessed that despite all I have, what I've given, what I've experienced, how I've lived, the plans I made and delivered, the one thing I really couldn't do without, and I suppose we all want is; **To be loved**.